Every Thing That Grows

Bob Chilcott

for SATB, clarinet, and piano

Clarinet part

Duration: *c.*7 minutes

CLARINET in B♭

Commissioned by the West Point Glee Club, United States Military Academy;
Constance Chase, Director

Every Thing That Grows

BOB CHILCOTT

With breadth and strength ♩ = c.72

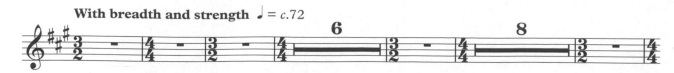

When I per-ceive __ that men as plants in-crease,

Pno.

_p_ espress.

_mp_

Then the con-ceit of this in-con-stant stay

Duration: 7 mins

Printed in Great Britain

BC170 **Every Thing That Grows** CHILCOTT

OXFORD
UNIVERSITY PRESS

www.oup.com

ISBN 978-0-19-341367-2

9 780193 413672